MW01594965

Religious Freedom in America

Edited by A. J. Scopino, Jr.

*This cartoon portrays New World Puritans debating
whether or not to cleanse religion of frivilous customs
such as "Old Christmas."*

Discovery Enterprises, Ltd.
Carlisle, Massachusetts

© Discovery Enterprises, Ltd., Carlisle, MA 1997

ISBN 1-57960-026-3 paperback edition
Library of Congress Catalog Card Number 97-77597

10 9 8 7 6 5 4 3 2 1

Printed in the United States of America

Subject Reference Guide:

The Struggle for Religious Freedom in America
edited by A. J. Scopino, Jr.

Religion in America — U. S. History

Religious Persecution — U. S. History

Jews in America — U. S. History

African Islam in America — U. S. History

Illustration/Photo Credits:

Cover art: Cartoon by Thomas Nast, illustrating separation of church and state, with government turning away the appeals of churches to be the "National Religion."

All other illustration and photo credits appear in the text.

Editor's notes regarding the documents:
1. *All original spelling has been retained.*
2. *A full line of dots indicates the deletion of at least an entire paragraph.*

Table of Contents

Introduction

by
A. J. Scopino, Jr.

"Congress shall make no law respecting an establishment of religion, or prohibiting the free exercise thereof..."

— Bill of Rights, First Amendment, 1791

"...No state shall make or enforce any law which shall abridge the privileges or immunities of citizens of the United States; nor shall any state deprive any person of life, liberty, or property, without due process of law, nor deny to any person within its jurisdiction the equal protection of the laws."

— Fourteenth Amendment, Section 1, 1868

The protection of one's freedom of religion is contained in these two amendments. On the one hand, the federal government, as indicated in the First Amendment, cannot interfere in the religious affairs of Americans. On the other hand, the states, as mandated by the Fourteenth Amendment, cannot make laws that deprive citizens of "life, liberty, or property." Liberty, in the context of the Fourteenth Amendment, includes the freedom to follow one's conscience in matters of religion. Buttressed by these safeguards, Americans have enjoyed one of the most cherished of civil liberties, that of religious freedom. Yet, constitutional guarantees notwithstanding, some religious groups, in the course of the nation's history, have been subject to unfair taxation, denied political rights, and have, at times, experienced outright violence.

Discrimination and persecution based upon religious grounds were part of the cultural baggage that accompanied the first settlers to North America. In fact, some of the first refugees who fled to these shores in search of religious freedom sought to insure their own religious supremacy by establishing a working arrangement between the church and civil authority. *Establishment*, as it was referred to, imposed a rigid conformity to the dictates of one church. This conformity was enforced by the coercive power of government. Together, church and state supported each other, imposing a rigid uniformity in political and religious affairs.

In New England, for example, the Puritan or Congregational church was established. In South Carolina, Virginia, Maryland, Georgia, and New York, the Church of England, also referred to as the Anglican or Episcopal church, was established. Anglicans were also influential in the middle colonies. While the union of church and state sought to impose religious uniformity, in many instances the complete opposite resulted. Resentment among those who disagreed with established churches continued to grow as the repressive side of government subjected dissenters, or those who disagreed with established churches, to taxation, public whippings, banishment, and even death. In 1660, three Quakers were hanged on Boston Common after they defied an order not to return to the city.

In spite of the exclusionary practices of established religious groups, the American colonies had been from earliest times a multi-religious society. Anglicans in the South, Puritans in New England, Roman Catholics in Maryland, a host of German pietists in the middle colonies, Quakers in Pennsylvania, Dutch Reformed and Lutherans in New York, pockets of Jews throughout the colonies, all made colonists generally aware of the remarkable religious diversity that surrounded them. Confronted with such diversity, colonists had grown accustomed to religious dissent. In time, the very foundation of establishment would begin to crumble under the weight of this ever-growing religious pluralism.

There were three reasons why established religion would begin to weaken and ultimately fall. First, the proliferation of religious groups often went unchecked by local governing bodies. Dissenters could flourish in the rural hinterland and remain out of harm's way. At times, albeit reluctantly, local authorities extended a grudging tolerance to dissenters. Dissenters, although still subject to political restrictions and still responsible for the financial support of the reigning establishment, could survive existing on the margins of society as, what historian R. Lawrence Moore has called, "religious outsiders."

The second development occurred within the realm of politics. As American colonists began to question British rule in the 1760s and 1770s, there developed a consciousness of democratic ideals that directly challenged British authoritarianism in all its forms — whether it be taxation without representation, unfair trade policies, or supporting British war efforts. This challenge to political authority soon began to overlap into religious matters as well. Freedom of conscience, now heralded as a democratic ideal, began to meld forcefully with political independence.

The third development which weakened the establishment principle was "enlightenment" thought. This thinking promoted the use of reason, called for free inquiry into matters secular and sacred, often promoted skepticism with regard to organized religion, and, at times, generated an intense anti-clericalism. The dissemination of such ideas empowered colonists not only to challenge orthodox religious beliefs but also to question the nature of, and justification for, established churches. Such thinking further promoted an already growing democratic ideology, which encompassed both political and religious thinking.

These three developments ostensibly did much to weaken all vestiges of authoritarian rule, whether they be religious or political. Consequently, in the highly-charged egalitarian climate of late eighteenth-century America, there arose a conscious effort to reach beyond mere toleration and promote the cause of *complete* freedom of religion.

With the winning of independence from Great Britain by 1783, the new nation began to dismantle the country's religious establishments.

Inspired by the efforts and writings of Thomas Jefferson and James Madison of Virginia, as well as by many dissenting bodies, the concept of an established church gradually lost favor. In keeping with the democratic spirit, virtually all of the new states began to delete restrictive clauses regarding religion from their constitutions. Now, in most states, churches were placed on an equal footing with one another and supported by the voluntary offerings of their constituents. This "democratization of religion," as historian Nathan Hatch has called it, was an ancillary outcome of the American Revolution. The concept of voluntarism had replaced establishment. Some states, however, moved more slowly toward granting full religious liberty. Connecticut and Massachusetts, for example, stubbornly resisted efforts to disestablish Congregationalism until 1818 and 1833, respectively.

With the disappearance of establishment within the first third of the nineteenth century, and with freedom of conscience seemingly in place, religious discontent, nonetheless, persisted.

African Muslim slaves continued to be subject to forced conversion by Christian groups in an effort to eradicate all cultural Africanisms, including religion. The Church of Latter Day Saints, the Mormons, felt the brunt of religious violence for their unorthodox religious beliefs and were driven west to the safety of the Utah territory. Roman Catholic and Jewish immigrants arriving in the latter decades of the nineteenth and early decades of the twentieth centuries, would suffer political, social, and economic discrimination. Native American religious rituals, regarded as heathen practice by many, prompted some whites to take measures to extirpate all traces of tribal religion. Even within Christianity itself, disagreement over theology and social issues often led to schism, or division, within churches. Thus, neither the guarantee of religious freedom nor the coming of a more modern egalitarian-conscious era could completely quiet the clamor of religious intolerance.

In more recent times, questions concerning religious freedom have presented the courts with constitutional dilemmas. Can religious missionaries canvass neighborhoods in an attempt to proselytize, even when the doctrines they espouse are hurtful and obnoxious to members of other religious groups? Should prayer be permitted in public schools? Should restrictions be enforced on Appalachian snake-handlers who use venomous serpents during worship services? Should some religions, such as the Native American Church of North America, which has used the hallucinogen, peyote, in religious ceremonies since pre-Columbian times, be permitted to continue such practices? Should members of certain religious groups such as Quakers, Amish, Black Muslims, and others, be excused from military duty for religious reasons? The answers to these questions are complex. These questions also involve a broader understanding of religious freedom, one far more comprehensive than our Constitution provides.

Unfortunately, the Constitution's vagueness frustrates any search for definitive guidelines in matters of religion in general, and religious freedom in particular. Constitutional historian Lawrence W. Levy has informed us that the framers of the Bill of Rights were either purposely vague or downright careless. The document offers little as to specifics, which, in turn, necessitates a great deal of interpretation by the courts. The dilemmas posed by these questions have forced legal experts, jurists, religious leaders, and government officials to undertake new readings of our constitutional guarantees and often require fresh interpretations.

The government's attempt to remain faithful to the constitutional provisions guaranteeing our religious liberties, by steadfastly maintaining a position of neutrality in matters of religion, has proved to be no simple task. The freedom to follow one's conscience in matters of religion has been one of America's most treasured liberties. At the same time, maintaining religious freedom in a judicious manner for all Americans has been a difficult undertaking.

The following excerpts from autobiographies, letters, newspapers, legislative documents, court decisions, observations by foreign visitors, and other accounts, highlight some of the key issues and events of the struggle for religious freedom in America.

Colonists Struggle with Religion

Theocracy in New England

One of the staunchest advocates of a union between church and state was the Puritan minister John Cotton (1584-1652). Cotton was not hesitant in barring unbelievers, that is non-Puritans, from holding public office or in denying them positions of influence in any manner. A firm believer in theocracy, Cotton believed that only the "saints" could be entrusted with the reins of power in both church and state. In the sermon attributed to him below, Cotton leaves no uncertainty as to who should govern and as to the danger of sharing civil power with non-believers. The language of the document has been modified by this editor for a more fluent reading.

Source: John Cotton, "A Discourse About Civil Government," in *Church and State in American History.* Englewood, N.J.: D.C. Heath and Company, 1965, p. 7.

...And...that those free burgesses have the only power of choosing from among themselves civil magistrates and men to be entrusted with transacting all public affairs of importance according to the rules and directions of Scripture?

I hold the affirmative....

Argument 1: Theocracy, [a form of government in which God or a deity is considered to be the supreme ruler] or to make the Lord God our governor, is the best form of government in a Christian commonwealth, and...men who are free to choose...ought to establish [it]....That form of government where, (a) the people who have the power of choosing their governors are in covenant [Every believer in Puritan New England was expected to enter into a covenant, or contract, in his heart with God, promising to obey His commandments and other directives as outlined within Scripture.] with God, (b) wherein the men chosen by them are godly men and fitted with a spirit of government, (c) in which laws they rule are the laws of God, (d) wherein laws are executed, inheritances allotted, and civil differences are composed according to God's appointment, [and] (e) in which men of God are consulted [about] all hard cases and in matters of religion, [this] is the form which was received and established among the people of Israel while the Lord God was their governor.

Argument 2: The form of government which gives unto Christ his due preeminence is the best form of government in a Christian commonwealth....

Argument 3: That form of government [in which] the best provision is made for the good both of the church and of the civil state is the best form of a government in a Christian communion....

Argument 4: That form of government [in which] the power of civil administration is denied unto unbelievers and [is] committed to the saints is the best form of government in a Christian Commonwealth....

Argument 5: That form of government [in which] the power of choosing from among themselves men to be entrusted with managing all public affairs of importance is committed to those who are furnished with the best helps for securing to a Christian state the full discharge of such a trust is the best form of government in a Christian Commonwealth....

Argument 6: [There is a danger of devolving power upon those not members of the church.]

It seems to be a principle imprinted in the minds and hearts of all men in the equity of it that such a form of government as best serves to establish their religion should, by the consent of all, be established in the civil state.

Challenge to Orthodoxy

Nearly a decade after his expulsion from the Massachusetts Bay Colony in 1635, Roger Williams (1603-1683) penned his thoughts on freedom of conscience in what became his most famous work, "The Bloudy Tenent of Persecution for Cause of Conscience." Originally written in 1644 in dialogue form between Truth and Peace, the work is in essence a repudiation of Puritan political thought and defines a clear separation of powers between church and state. The work was considered so radical that Parliament ordered the document to be publicly burned. In the pursuit of religious freedom,Williams went on to found the Providence settlement in what became the colony of Rhode Island. Here, as in Pennsylvania later, religious tolerance was enjoyed by most. In fact, the colony's acceptance of the varied array of believers irritated Massachusetts Bay Puritans so much, they often referred to the new colony as "Rogues Island."

Source: Roger Williams, "The Bloudy Tenent of Persecution for Cause of Conscience," in Edmund S. Morgan, ed., *Puritan Political Ideas, 1558-1794.* Indianapolis: The Bobbs-Merrill Company, Inc., 1965, pp. 198-200, originally published in London, 1644.

...the proper meanes whereby the Civill Power may and should attaine its end are only Politicall, and principally these Five.

First, the erecting and establishing what forme of Civill Government may seeme in wisedom most meet, according to general rules of the Word, and the state of the people.

Secondly, the making, publishing, and establishing of wholesome Civill Lawes, not only such as concerne Civill Justice, but also the free passage of true Religion: for outward Civill Peace ariseth and is maintained from them both, from the latter as well as from the former:

Civill peace cannot stand intire, where Religion is corrupted....And yet such Lawes, though conversant about Religion, may still be counted Civill Lawes, as on the contrary, an Oath doth still remaine Religious, though conversant about Civill matters.

Thirdly, Election and appointment of Civill officers, to see execution of those Lawes.

Fourthly, Civill Punishments and Rewards, of Transgressors and Observers of these Lawes.

Fifthly, taking up Armes against the Enemies of Civill Peace.

...the meanes whereby the Church may and should attaine her ends, are only ecclesiastical, which are chiefly five.

First, setting up that forme of Church Government only, of which Christ hath given them a pattern in his Word.

Secondly, acknowledging and admitting of no Lawgiver in the Church, but Christ, and the publishing of his Lawes.

Thirdly, electing and ordaining of such officers onely, as Christ hath appointed in his Word.

Fourthly, to receive into their fellowship them that are approved, and inflicting Spirituall censures against them that offend.

Fifthly, Prayer and patience in suffering any evill from them that be without, who disturbe the peace.

So that Magistrates, as Magistrates, have no power of setting up the Forme of Church Government, electing Church officers, punishing with Church censures, but to see that the Church doth her duty herein. And on the other side, the Churches as Churches, have no power (though as members of the Commonweale they may have power) of erecting or altering formes of Civill Government, electing of Civill officers, inflicting Civill punishments (no not on persons excommunicate) as by deposing Magistrates from their Civill Authoritie, or withdrawing the hearts of people against them, to their Lawes, no more then to discharge wives, or children, or servants, from due obedience to their husbands, parents, or masters: or by taking up armes against their Magistrates, though he persecute them for Conscience: for though members of Churches who are publique officers also of the Civill State, may suppresse by force the violence of Usurpers,...yet this they doe not as members of the Church, but as officers of the Civill State.

Liberty of Conscience

While aimed at those who persecuted Quakers in England, William Penn's (1644-1718) "The Great Case for Liberty of Conscience" (1670), clearly set forth the author's stand on freedom of conscience. The document served as a guiding principle for the founding of the Quaker colony of Pennsylvania, where religious freedom was far more widespread.

Source: Frederick B. Tolles and E. Gordon Alderfer, eds., *The Witness of William Penn*. New York: The Macmillan Company, 1959, pp. 69-71, originally published as *The Great Case for Liberty of Conscience Once More Briefly Debated and Defended.* Newgate, 1670.

...By Liberty of Conscience, we understand not only a mere Liberty of the Mind, in believing or disbelieving this or that principle or doctrine; but the "exercise of ourselves in a visible way of worship, upon our believing it to be indispensably required at our hands, that if we neglect it for fear or favour of any mortal man, we sin, and incur divine wrath." Yet we would be so understood to extend and justify the lawfulness of our meeting to worship God, as not to contrive, or abet any contrivance destructive of the government and the laws of the land, tending to matters of an external nature directly or indirectly; but so far as it may refer to religious matters, and a life to come, and consequently wholly independent of the secular affairs of this, wherein we are supposed to transgress.

...By imposition, restraint, and persecution, we do not only mean the strict requiring of us to believe this to be true, or that to be false; and upon refusal, to incur the penalties enacted in such cases; but by those terms we mean thus much, "any coercive lett or hindrance to us; from meeting together to perform those religious exercises which are according to our faith and persuasion."

....

...Then we say, that Imposition, Restraint, and Persecution, for matters relating to conscience, directly invade the divine prerogative, and divest the Almighty of a due, proper to none besides himself.

...If we allow the honour of our creation due to God only, and that no other besides himself has endowed us with those excellent gifts of

Understanding, Reason, Judgment, and Faith, and consequently that he only is the object, as well as the author, both of our faith, Worship, and Service; the whosoever shall interpose their authority to enact faith and worship in a way that seems not to us congruous with what he has discovered to us to be faith and worship...or to restrain us from what we are persuaded is our indispensable duty, they evidently usurp this authority, and invade his incommunicable right of government over conscience....

...Such magisterial determinations carry an evident claim to that infallibility, which Protestants have been hitherto so jealous of owning....

...It enthrones man as king over conscience, the alone just claim and privilege of his Creator; whose thoughts are not as mens thoughts, but has reserved to himself that empire from all the Caesars on earth....

Painting of a Quaker meeting
(Courtesy of the Museum of Fine Arts, Boston, MA)

...It defeats God's work of Grace, and the invisible operation of his eternal Spirit,...and attributes mens conformity to outward force and corporal punishments. A faith subject to as many revolutions as the powers that enact it.

...Such persons assume the judgment of the great tribunal unto themselves; in them; for to whomsoever men are imposedly or restrictively subject and accountable in matters of faith, worship and conscience; in them alone must the power of judgment reside; but it is equally true that God shall judge all by Jesus Christ; and that no man is so accountable to his fellow-creatures, as to be imposed upon, restrained, or persecuted for any matter of conscience whatever.

The Toleration Act of 1649 - Maryland

Founded as a refuge for English Roman Catholics in 1634, Maryland codified religious toleration for all Christians with the passage of the Toleration Act of 1649. Scheming and jealousy brought an end to religious freedom for Roman Catholics in the early 1650s when a group of Protestants seized political control of the colony. While Catholics retained their lands and estates, they were denied public office. Below is an excerpt from the act of 1649, outlining the specifics of toleration.

Source: Matthew Page Andrews, *History of Maryland: Province and State.* New York: Doubleday, Doran & Company, Inc., 1929, pp. 697-699.

Forasmuch as in a well-governed and Christian commonwealth, matters concerning religion and the honour of our God ought in the first place to bee taken into serious consideration, and indevoured to bee settled, Bee it therefore ordayned and enacted by the right honourable Cecilius lord baron of Baltimore, absolute lord and proprietary of this province, with the advice and consent of the upper and lower house of this general assembly, that whatsoever person or persons within this province and the islands thereunto belonging, shall from henceforth blaspheme God, that is, to curse him, or shall deny our Saviour Jesus Christ to be the Son of God, or shall deny the Holy Trinity, the Father, Son, and Holy Ghost, or the Godhead, or any of the sayd Three Persons of the Trinity, or the Unity of the Godhead, or shall use or utter any reproachful speeches, words or languages concerning the Holy Trinity, or any of the sayd three persons thereof, shall be punished with death, and confiscation or forfeiture of all his or her land and goods to the lord proprietary and his heires.

....

And be it also further enacted by the same Authority, advice and assent, that whosoever person or persons shall from henceforth upon any occasion of offense or otherwise in a reproachful manner of way, declare, call or denominate any persons or persons, whosoever inhabiting, residing, trafficking, trading or commercing, within this province, or within any of the ports, harbour, creeks, or havens, to the same belonging, an Heretick, Schismatic, Idolator, Puritan, Presbyterian, Independent, Popish Priest, Jesuit, Jesuited Priest, Lutheran, Calvinist, Anabaptist, Brownist, Anitnomian, Barrowist, Roundhead, Separatist, or other name or terme in a reproachful manner, relating to a matter of religion, shall for every such offense forfeit and lose 10 pounds sterling, or the value thereof to be levied on the goods and chattels of every such offender or offenders, the one half thereof to be forfeited and paid unto the person or persons of who such reproachful words are or shall be spoken or uttered and the other halfe to the lord proprietary and his heirs....

....

And whereas the inforcing of the conscience in matters of religion hath frequently fallen out to bee of dangerous consequence in those commonwealths where it hath beene practised, and for the more quiet and peaceable government of this province, and the better to preserve mutuall love and unity amongst the inhabitants here, Bee it therefore also by the lord proprietary with the advice and assent of this assembly ordained and enacted, except as in this present act is before declared and set forth, that no person or persons whatsoever within this province or the island, ports, harbours, creeks or havens thereunto belonging, professing to believe in Jesus Christ, shall henceforth be any waies troubled, molested, or discountenanced, for or in his or her religion, nor in the free exercise thereof...nor any way compelled to beleefe or exercise of any other religion against his or her consent,...that such person or persons so offending shall be compelled to pay treble damages to the party so wronged or molested....

Jefferson's Model for Religious Freedom

First introduced into the Virginia Assembly on June 13, 1779, and finally adopted in 1786, the Bill for Establishing Religious Freedom would be considered by many to be Thomas Jefferson's (1743-1826) greatest achievement and would serve as a model for the rest of the country. A member of the Episcopal Church, Jefferson's personal religion was founded upon enlightenment principles such as reason, good works, toleration, and free inquiry. In the following excerpt from the Bill for Establishing Religious Freedom, Jefferson underscores freedom of conscience as a natural right.

Source: CONSTITUTION, Volume 7 No.1, Foundation for the United States Constitution. New York: 1995, p. 23.

Section I. Whereas Almighty God hath created the mind free; that all attempts to influence it by temporal punishments, or burthens, or by civil incapacitations, tend only to beget habits of hypocrisy and meanness, and are a departure from the plan of the Holy author of our religion, who being Lord both of body and mind, yet choose not to propagate it by coercions on either, as was in his Almighty power to do; that the impious presumption of legislators and rulers, civil as well as ecclesiastical, who being themselves but fallible and uninspired men, have assumed dominion over the faith of others, setting up their own opinions and modes of thinking as the only true and infallible, and as such endeavoring to impose them on others, hath established and maintained false religions over the greatest part of the world, and through all time; that to compel a man to furnish contributions of money for the propagation of opinions which he disbelieves, is sinful and tyrannical; that even the forcing him to support this or that teacher of his own religious persuasion, is depriving him of the comfortable liberty of giving his contributions to the particular pastor of whose morals he would make his pattern, and whose powers he feels most persuasive to righteousness, and is withdrawing from the ministry those temporary rewards, which proceeding from an approbation of their personal conduct, are an additional incitement to earnest and unremitting labours for the instruction of mankind; that our civil rights have no dependence on our religious opinions, any more than our opinions in physics or geometry; that therefore the proscribing any citizen as unworthy the public confidence by laying upon him an incapacity of being called to offices of trust...unless he profess or renounce this or that religious opinion, is depriving him injuriously of those privileges and advantages to which, in common with his fellow-citizens, he has a natural right...that to suffer the civil magistrate to intrude his powers into the field of opinion, and to restrain the profession or propagation of principles on supposition of their ill tendency is a dangerous fallacy, which at once destroys all religious liberty....

Section II. Be it enacted by the General Assembly, that no man shall be compelled to frequent or support any religious worship, place, or ministry whatsoever, nor shall be enforced, restrained, molested, or burthened in his body or goods, nor shall otherwise suffer, on account of his religious opinions or belief; but that all men shall be free to profess, and by argument to maintain, their opinions in matters of religion, and that the same shall in no wise diminish, enlarge, or affect their civil capacities.

Section III. And though we well know that this Assembly, elected by the people for the ordinary purposes of legislation only, have no power to restrain the acts of succeeding assemblies, constituted with powers equal to our own, and that therefore to declare this act to be irrevocable would be of no effect in law; yet we are free to declare, and do declare, that the rights hereby asserted are of the natural rights of mankind, and that if any act shall be hereafter passed to repeal the present or to narrow its operations, such act will be an infringement of natural rights.

Fending Off Establishment in Virginia

Miniature of James Madison in 1776,
by Charles Wilson Peale (Courtesy of the Library of Congress)

Reacting to a bill that would have initiated state support for the mainte-
nance of the Episcopal clergy in Virginia, James Madison (1751-1836) fired
off "A Memorial and Remonstrance," which successfully argued in favor of
the separation between church and state. Like his fellow Virginian, Thomas
Jefferson, Madison remained suspect of any alliance between civil govern-
ment and religious bodies. Below Madison outlines his arguments against
the support for "Teachers of the Christian Religion."

Source: James Madison, "A Memorial and Remonstrance," in Marvin Myers, ed., *The
Mind of the Founder: Sources of the Political Thought of James Madison*, rev. ed. Hanover,
New Hampshire: University Press of New England, 1981, pp. 6-12.

We, the subscribers, citizens of the said Commonwealth, having
taken into serious consideration, a Bill printed by order of the last
Session of General Assembly, entitled "A Bill establishing a provision for Teachers of the Christian Religion," and conceiving that the
same, if finally armed with the sanctions of a law, will be a dangerous abuse of power, are bound as faithful members of a free State, to

21

remonstrate against it, and to declare the reasons by which we are determined. We remonstrate against the said Bill,

1. ...The Religion then of every man must be left to the conviction and conscience of every man; and it is the right of every man to exercise it as these may dictate. This right is in its nature an unalienable right. It is unalienable; because the opinions of men, depending only on the evidence contemplated by their own minds, cannot follow the dictates of other men: It is unalienable also, because what is here a right toward men, is a duty towards the Creator. It is the duty of every man to render to the Creator such homage, and such only, as he believes to be acceptable to him....We maintain therefore that in matters of Religion, no man's right is abridged by the institution of Civil Society, and that Religion is wholly exempt from its cognizance.

2. Because if religion be exempt from the authority of the Society at large, still less can it be subject to that of the Legislative Body. The latter are but creatures and vice regents of the former. Their jurisdiction is both derivative and limited: it is limited with regard to the co-ordinate departments, more necessarily is it limited with regard to the constituents.

3. Because, it is proper to take alarm at the first experiment on our liberties. We hold this prudent jealousy to be the first duty of citizens, and one of [the] noblest characteristics of the late Revolution....Who does not see that the same authority which can establish Christianity, in exclusion of all other Religions, may establish with the same ease any particular sect of Christians, in exclusion of all other Sects?

4. ...Whilst we assert for ourselves a freedom to embrace, to profess and to observe the Religion which we be-

lieve to be of divine origin, we cannot deny an equal freedom to those whose minds have not yet yielded to the evidence which has thus convinced us. If this freedom be abused, it is an offense against God, not against man; To God, therefore, not to men, must an account of it be rendered.

....

7. Because experience witnesseth that ecclesiastical establishments, instead of maintaining the purity and efficacy of Religion, have had a contrary operation. During almost fifteen centuries, has the legal establishment of Christianity been on trial. What have been its fruits? More or less in all places, pride and indolence in the Clergy; ignorance and servility in the laity; in both, superstition, bigotry and persecution.

....

11. Because it will destroy that moderation and harmony which the forbearance of our laws to intermeddle with Religion, has produced amongst its several sects. Torrents of blood have been split in the old world, by vain attempts of the secular arm to extinguish Religious discord, by proscribing all difference in Religious opinions.

....

15. Because, finally, "the equal right of every citizen to the free exercise of his Religion according to the dictates of conscience" is held by the same tenure with all our other rights.

Jews in America

One of the world's religious groups that has suffered throughout history has been the Jews. In the North American colonies, the situation was often the same. Colonial constitutions often prevented Jews from gaining a foothold in the colonies and petitions by Jews for the opportunity to settle were routinely turned down. The following selections illustrate the difficulty Jews experienced in early America.

Peter Stuyvesant Requests Permission to Expel Jews From New Amsterdam, 1654

Source: Michael Selzer, ed., *"Kike!" —Anti-Semitism in America*. New York: World Publishing, 1972, pp. 10, 13-14, originally published in Samuel Oppenheim, "The Early History of the Jews in New York, 1654-1664," *Publications of the American Jewish Historical Society*, XVIII (1909).

The Jews who have arrived would nearly all like to remain here, but learning that they (with their customary usury and deceitful trading with the Christians) were very repugnant to the inferior magistrates, as also to the people having the most affection for you; the Deaconry also fearing that owing to their present indigence they might become a charge in the coming winter, we have, for the benefit of this weak and newly developing place and the land in general, deemed it useful to require them in a friendly way to depart; praying also most seriously in this connection, for ourselves as also for the general community of your worships, that the deceitful race—such hateful enemies and blasphemers of the name of Christ—be not allowed to further infect and trouble this new colony to the detraction of your worships and the dissatisfaction of your worships' most affectionate subjects.

Jews are Denied Naturalization in Rhode Island, 1762

Although the Jews did not have smooth sailing in colonial America, they were accepted in Rhode Island, despite being denied naturalization in 1762. An excerpt from the denial of the naturalization of Aaron Lopez and Isaac Elizer follows.

Source: Franklin B. Dexter, *Extracts from the Itineraries and Other Miscellanies of Ezra Stiles, D.D., LL.D., 1755-1794.* New Haven, 1916.

The petition of Messrs Aaron Lopez and Isaac Elizer, persons professing the Jewish religion, praying that they may be naturalized on an act of Parliament made in the 13th year of His Majesty's reign George the Second, having been duly considered, and also the act of Parliament therein referred to, this court are unanimously of the opinion that the said act of Parliament was widely designed for increasing the number of inhabitants in the plantations; but this colony being already so full of people that many of His Majesty's good subjects born within the same have removed and settled in Nova Scotia and other places; [the petition] cannot come within the intention of the said act.

Further, by the charter granted to this colony, it appears that the full and quiet enjoyment of the Christian religion and a desire of propagating the same were the principal views with which the colony was settled; and by a law made and passed in the year 1663, no person who does not profess the Christian religion can be admitted free of this colony. This court therefore unanimously dismiss the said petition as absolutely inconsistent with the first principle upon which the colony was founded and with a law now of the same in full force.

The Expulsion of the Jews from Georgia, 1764

The Trustees of Colonial Georgia wanted Jews removed in 1764.

Source: Charles C. Jones, Jr., *History of Savannah, Georgia.* Syracuse, 1890.

———————————————————————————

Ordered.   That the Secretary do wait on Messrs. Alvaro Lopez Suassa, Francis Salvador, Jr., and Anthony DaCosta with the following Message in writing:

> The Trustees for establishing the Colony of Georgia in America having receiv'd a letter from Messrs. Alvaro Lopez Suassa, Francis Salvador, Jr. and Anthony DaCosta, in answer to a message sent for their Commissions, which letter does not appear satisfactory to the said Trustees, they think themselves oblig'd not only to insist on the redelivery of their Commissions, but as they conceive of the settling of Jews in Georgia will be prejudicial to the Colony, and as some have been sent without the knowledge of the Trustees, the Trustees do likewise require that the said Messrs. Alvaro Lopez Suassa, Francis Salvador, Jr. and Anthony DaCosta, or whoever else may have been concerned in sending them over, do use their endeavors that the said Jews may be removed from the Colony of Georgia, as the best and only satisfaction they can give to the Trustees for such an indignity offer'd to Gentlemen acting under His Majesty's Charter.

The First Synagogue in America

Jews completed the first synagogue in America in 1763. It still stands today on Touro Street in Newport, Rhode Island

Photo by John T. Hopf

The interior of Touro Synagogue
(Courtesy of Society of Friends of Touro Synagogue)

Washington's Letter to the Jewish Community of New Port, Rhode Island, 1790

In the following account, President George Washington sends a letter of appreciation to the Jewish community in Newport, Rhode Island, for the welcome he received upon a visit to that city in 1790. Included in Washington's message is a statement concerning the freedom of conscience and the evils of religious persecution. The contents of the President's message marked a departure in the attitude of American Christians toward Jews.

Source: Morris U. Shappes, ed., *A Documentary History of the Jews in the United States 1654-1875*, rev. ed. New York: The Citadel Press, 1952, pp. 80-81, originally published in *Washington Papers*, Library of Congress, 19-20.

Gentlemen:

While I receive with much satisfaction your address replete with expressions of affection and esteem; I rejoice in the opportunity of assuring you that I shall always retain a grateful remembrance of the cordial welcome I experienced in my visit to New Port from all classes of Citizens.

The reflection on the days of difficulty and danger which are past is rendered the more sweet from a consciousness that they are succeeded by days of uncommon prosperity and security. If we have wisdom to make the best use of the advantages with which we are now favored, we cannot fail, under the just administration of a good government to become a great and happy people.

The Citizens of the United States of America have a right to applaud themselves for having given to mankind examples of an enlarged and liberal policy, a policy worthy of imitation.

All possess alike liberty of conscience and immunities of citizenship. It is now no more that toleration is spoken of, as if it was by the indulgence of one class of people, that another enjoyed the exercise of their natural rights. For happily the government of the United States, which gives to bigotry no sanction, to persecution no assistance, requires only that they who live under its protection should demean themselves as good citizens, in giving it on all occasions their effectual support.

It would be inconsistent with the frankness of my character not to avow that I am pleased with your favorable opinion of my administration, and fervent wishes for my felicity.

May the children of the Stock of Abraham, who dwell in this land, continue to merit and enjoy the good will of the other inhabitants, while every one shall sit in safety under his own vine and fig-tree, and there shall be none to make him afraid.

May the Father of all mercies scatter light and not darkness in our paths, and make us all in our several vocations useful here, and in his own time and way everlastingly happy.

G. Washington

The Tide Turns

The Emergence of Rational Religion

One of the most powerful writers of the late eighteenth century was the Englishman Thomas Paine (1737-1809), free-thinker, political polemicist, and devoted revolutionary. It was from Paine's political writings which American revolutionaries drew inspiration in their quest for independence. In 1794 Paine published The Age of Reason, *a devastating attack on organized religion. The book attacked the repressive side of religious orthodoxy and the danger it posed to an enlightened and informed citizenry. In the following selection Paine establishes the essentials of his simplified faith, and the primacy of reason over revelation.*

Source: Eric Foner, ed., *Paine: Collected Writings.* New York: Library Classics of America, 1995, pp. 66-68, originally published as *The Age of Reason: Being an Investigation of True and Fabulous Theology*, Paris, 1794.

I believe in one God, and no more; and I hope for happiness beyond this life.

I believe the equality of man, and I believe that religious duties consist in doing justice, loving mercy, and endeavor to make our fellow creatures happy.

But lest it should be supposed that I believe many other things in addition to these, I shall, in the progress of this work, declare the things I do not believe, and my reasons for not believing them.

I do not believe in the creed professed by the Jewish church, by the Roman church, by the Greek church, by the Turkish church, by the Protestant church, not by any church that I know of. My own mind is my own church.

All national institutions of churches, whether Jewish, Christian, or Turkish, appear to me no other than human inventions set up to terrify and enslave mankind, and monopolize power and profit.

I do not believe by this declaration to condemn those who believe otherwise. They have the same right to their beliefs as I have to mine. But it is necessary to the happiness of man, that he be mentally faithful to himself. Infidelity does not consist in believing, or in disbelieving: it consists in professing to believe what he does not believe.

....

Every national church or religion has established itself by pretending some special mission from God communicated to certain individuals. The Jews have their Moses; the Christians have their Jesus Christ, their apostles and saints; and the Turks their Mahomet; as if the way to God was open to every man alike.

Each of those churches show certain books which they call *revelation*, or the word of God. The Jews say that their word of God was given by God to Moses face to face; the Christians say, that their word of God came by divine inspiration; and the Turks say, that their word of God [the Koran] was brought by an angel from heaven. Each of those churches accuses the other of unbelief; and, for my own part, I disbelieve them all.

As it is necessary to affix right ideas to words, I will, before I proceed further into the subject, offer some observations on the word *revelation*. Revelation, when applied to religion, means something communicated *immediately* from God to man.

No one will deny or dispute the power of the Almighty to make such a communication if he pleases. But admitting, for the sake of a case, that something has been revealed to a certain person, and not revealed to any other person, it is revelation to that person only. When he tells it to a second person, a second to a third, a third to a fourth, and so on [it] ceases to be a revelation to all those persons. It is revelation to the first person only, and *hearsay* to every other; and consequently, they are not obliged to believe it.

The Connecticut Establishment Falls

One of the most influential and popular clergymen in the ante-bellum period was Lyman Beecher (1775-1863). Born in Litchfield, Connecticut and the father of thirteen children, many of whom would follow him into the ministry, Beecher became involved in many pre-Civil War crusades, including the abolition of slavery and temperance reform. A staunch Federalist and Congregationalist minister, Beecher would mourn the day, in 1818, when the Congregational Church in Connecticut was disestablished. In the auto-biographical excerpt that follows, Beecher discusses the pain he experienced at the time of disestablishment.

Source: Barbara M. Cross, ed., *The Autobiography of Lyman Beecher.* Cambridge: Harvard University Press, 1961, pp. 251-253.

The efforts we made to execute the laws and secure a reformation of morals reached the men of piety, and waked up the energies of the whole state, so far as the members of our churches, and the intelligent and moral portion of our congregations were concerned. These, however, proved to be a minority of the suffrage of the state. Originally all were obliged to support the standing order. Everybody paid without kicking....

When, however, other denominations began to rise, and complained of their consciences, the laws were modified. There never was a more noble regard to the rights of conscience than was shown in Connecticut. Never was there a body of men that held the whole power that yielded to the rights of conscience more honorably.

The habit of legislation from the beginning had been to favor the Congregational order and provide for it. Congregationalism was the established religion. All others were dissenters and complained of favoritism. The ambitious minority early began to make use of the minor sects on the ground of invidious distinctions, thus making them restive. So the democracy, as it arose, included nearly all the minor sects, besides the Sabbath-breakers, rum-selling tippling folk, infidels, and ruff-scuff generally, and make a dead set at us of the standing order.

It was a long time, however, before they could accomplish any thing, so small were the sects and so united the Federal phalanx. After defeat upon defeat, and while other state delegations in Congress divided, ours, for twenty years a unit, Pierpont Edwards, a leader of the Democrats, exclaimed, "As well attempt to revolutionize the kingdom of heaven as the State of Connecticut!"

...persons of third-rate ability, on our side, who wanted to be somebody, deserted; all the infidels in the state had long been leading on that side; the minor sects had swollen, and complained of having to get a certificate to pay their tax where they liked; our efforts to enforce reformation of morals by law made us unpopular; they attacked the clergy unceasingly, and myself in particular, in season and out of season, with all sorts of misrepresentation, ridicule, and abuse; and finally the Episcopalians, who had always been staunch Federalists,...went over to the Democrats.

That overset us. They slung us out like a stone from a sling....

It was a long time of great depression and suffering. It was the worst attack I ever met in my life....I worked as hard as mortal man could, and at the same time preached for revivals with all my might, and with success, till at last, what with domestic afflictions and all, my health and spirits began to fail. It was as dark a day as I ever saw. The odium thrown upon the ministry was inconceivable. The injury done to the cause of Christ, as we then supposed, was irreparable. For several days I suffered what no tongue can tell *for the best thing that ever happened to the State of Connecticut.* It cut the churches loose from dependence on state support. It threw them wholly on their own resources and on God.

African Islam in America

Omar ibn Said (c. 1770-1859) was a West African taken into slavery in about 1806-1807. His autobiography, an account of about 2000 words written in 1831, is the only known slave account written in Arabic. A devout Muslim, who was highly educated, Ibn Said told of his life in Africa, his captivity, his coming to South Carolina, and his conversion experience at the hands of his master, Jim Owen. Conversions of African slaves to Christianity reflected an intolerance on the part of white masters who were eager to strip their chattels of any African cultural identity.

Source: "The Autobiography of Omar ibn Seid [Said]," *American Historical Review*, XXX, July, 1925, pp. 787-795.

My name is Omar ibn Seid. My birthplace was Fut Tur [modern day Senegal], between the two rivers. I sought knowledge under the instruction of a Sheikh called Mohammed Seid, my own brother, and Sheikh Soleiman Kembeh, and Sheikh Gabriel Abdal. I continued my studies twenty-five years, and then returned to my home where I remained six years. Then there came to our place a large army, who killed many men, and took me, and brought me to the great sea, and sold me into the hands of the Christians, who bound me and sent me on board a great ship and we sailed upon the great sea a month and a half, when we came to a place called Charleston [South Carolina] in the Christian language. Here they sold me to a small, weak, and wicked man called Johnson, a complete infidel, who had no fear of God at all. Now I am a small man, and unable to do hard work so I fled from the hand of Johnson and after a month came to a place called Fayd-il [Fayetteville]. There I saw some great houses [churches]. On the new moon I went into a church to pray. A lad saw me and rode off to the place of his father and informed him that he had seen a black man in the church. A man named Handah [Hunter?] and another man with him on horseback, came attended by a troop of dogs. They took me and made me go with them twelve miles to a place called Fayd-il, where they put me into a great house from which I could not go out. I continued in the great house (which in the Christian language they called jail) sixteen days and nights. One Friday the jailer came and opened the door of the house and I saw a great many men, all Christians, some of whom called out to me, "What is your name? It is Omar or Seid?" A man called Mumford took me and led me out of the jail, and I was very pleased to go with them to their place. I stayed at Mumford's four days and nights, and then a man named Jim Owen, son-in-law of Mumford,...asked if I was willing to go to a place called Bladen [Bladen County, North Carolina]. I said, Yes, I was willing. I went with them and have remained in the place of Jim Owen until now.

....

Before I came to the Christian country, my religion was the religion of "Mohammed, the Apostle of God—may God have mercy upon him and give him peace." I walked to the mosque before day-break, washed my face and hands and feet. I prayed at noon, prayed in the afternoon, prayed at sunset, prayed in the evening. I gave alms every year, gold, silver, seeds, cattle, sheep, goats, rice, wheat, and barley....When I left my country I was thirty-seven years old; I have been in the country of the Christians twenty-four years....

....

Formerly I, Omar, loved to read the book of the Koran....[The Koran is the holy book for those of the Islamic or Muslim faith.] General Jim Owen and his wife used to read the gospel, and they read it to me very much,—the gospel of God, our Lord, our Creator, our King, He that orders all our circumstances, health and wealth,...Open thou my heart to the gospel,....

....

When I was a Mohammedan I prayed thus: "Thanks be to God, Lord of all worlds, the merciful the gracious, Lord of the Judgment....But now I pray "Our Father", etc., in the words of our Lord Jesus the Messiah.

Europeans Observe American Religions

Mrs. Frances Trollope - 1832

One of the many European travelers to America in the early nineteenth century was Frances Milton Trollope (1780-1863), an English woman of leisure and refinement. Her travels throughout the nation were recorded in the Domestic Manners of the Americans, *published in 1832, a work that pleased and entertained English audiences. Her accounts of American lifestyles and cultural achievements were critical and derogatory. She found little of promise in American political life and social equality repulsed her. In the selection below, Mrs. Trollope discusses the shortcomings due to the lack of an established church and the danger in entrusting church administration to "every tinker and tailor." Clearly, Mrs. Trollope failed to appreciate the democratic qualities in American religion.*

Source: Frances Trollope, *Domestic Manners of the Americans*, ed., John Lauritz Larson. New York: Brandywine Press, 1993, pp. 63-65, originally published in London, 1832.

I had often heard it observed before I visited America, that one of the great blessings of its constitution was the absence of a national religion, the country being thus exonerated from all obligation of supporting the clergy; those only contributing to do so whose principles led them to it. My residence in the country has shewn me that a religious tyranny may be exerted very effectually without the aid of the government, in a way much more oppressive than the paying of the tithe, and without obtaining any of the salutary decorum, which I presume no one will deny is the result of an established mode of worship.

As it was impossible to remain many weeks in the country without being struck with the strange anomies produced by its religious system, my early notes contain many observations on the subject; but as nearly the same scenes recurred in every part of the country, I state them here, not as belonging to the west alone, but to the whole Union, the same cause producing the same effect every where.

The whole people appear to be divided into an almost endless variety of religious factions, and I was told, that to be well received in society, it was necessary to declare yourself as belonging to some one of these. Let your acknowledged belief be what it may, you are said to be not a Christian, unless you attach yourself to a particular congregation. Besides the broad and well-known distinctions of Episcopalian, Catholic, Presbyterian, Calvinist, Baptist, Quaker, Swedenborgian, Universalist, Dunker,...there are innumerable others springing out of these, each of which assumes a church government of its own; of this, the most intriguing and factious individual is invariably the head; and in order, as it should seem, to shew a reason for this separation, each congregation invests itself with some queer variety of external observance that has the melancholy effect of exposing all religious ceremonies to contempt.

It is impossible, in witnessing all these unseemly vagaries not to recognise the advantages of an established church as a sort of head-quarters for quiet unpresuming Christians, who are contented to serve faithfully, without insisting upon having each a little separate banner, embroidered with a device of their own imagining.

....

I believe I am sufficiently tolerant; but this does not prevent my seeing that the object of all religious observation is better obtained, when the government of the church is confided to the wisdom and experience of the most venerated among the people, than when it is placed in the hands of every tinker and tailor who chooses to claim a share in it. Nor is this the only evil attending the want of a national religion, supported by the State. As there is no legal and fixed provision for the clergy, it is hardly surprising that their services are confined to those who can pay them. The vehement expressions of insane or hypocritical zeal, such as were exhibited during "the Revival," can but ill atone for the want of village worship, any more than the eternal talk of the admirable and unequaled government, can atone for the continual contempt of social order. Church and State hobble along, side by side, notwithstanding their boasted independence. Almost every man you meet will tell you, that he is occupied in labours most abundant for the good of his country; and almost every woman will tell you, that besides those things that are within (her house) she has coming upon her daily the care of all the churches. Yet spite of this universal attention to the government, its laws are half asleep; and spite of the old women and their Dorcas societies, atheism is awake and thriving.

....

...It occurred to me, that in a country where "all men are equal," the government would be guilty of no great crime, did it so far interfere as to give them all *an opportunity* of becoming Christians if they wished it. But should the federal government dare to propose building a church, and endowing it, in some village...it is perfectly certain that not only the sovereign state where such an abomination was proposed, would rush into the Congress to resent the odious interference, but that all the other states would join the clamour, and such an intermeddling administration would run great risk of impeachment and degradation.

Alexis de Tocqueville - 1835

Alexis de Tocqueville (1805-1859) was one of many European visitors to tour the new nation and study its life, institutions, and culture. A member of the French aristocracy, Tocqueville, unlike Mrs. Trollope, found much to praise in American democracy. Democracy in America, *published in four volumes between 1835 and 1840, proved to be insightful to both Americans and Europeans alike. Below Tocqueville discusses the democratic aspects of American religion, particularly the equality of all religious groups and the distance between church and state.*

Source: Alexis de Tocqueville, *Democracy in America*, vol. I, ed. J.P. Mayer and Max Lerner. New York: Harper & Row, Publishers, 1966, pp. 267-269, originally published in Paris, 1835-1840.

There is an innumerable multitude of sects in the United states. They are all different in the worship they offer to the Creator, but all agree concerning the duties of men to one another. Each sect worships God in its own fashion, but all preach the same morality in the name of God. Though it is very important for man as an individual that his religion should be true, that is not the case for society. Society has nothing to fear or hope from another life; what is most important for it not that all citizens should profess the true religion but that they should profess religion. Moreover, all the sects in the United states belong to the great unity of Christendom, and Christian morality is everywhere the same.

One may suppose a certain number of Americans, in the worship they offer to God, are following their habits rather than their convictions. Besides, in the United states the sovereign authority is religious, and consequently hypocrisy should be common. Nonetheless, America is still the place where the Christian religion has kept the greatest power over men's souls; and nothing better demonstrates how useful and natural it is to man, since the country where it now has widest sway is both the most enlightened and the freest.

I have said that American priests proclaim themselves in general terms in favor of civil liberties without excepting even those who do not admit religious freedom; but none of them lend their support to any particular political system. They are at pains to keep out of affairs and not mix in the combinations of parties. One cannot therefore say that in the United States religion influences the laws or political opinions in detail....

....

Religion, which never intervenes directly in the government of American society, should therefore be considered as the first of their political institutions, for although it did not give them the taste for liberty, it singularly facilitates the use thereof.

The inhabitants of the United States themselves consider religious beliefs from this angle. I do not know if all Americans have faith in their religion—for who can read the secrets of the heart?—but I am sure that they think it necessary to the maintenance of republican institutions. That is not the view of one class or party among the citizens, but of the whole nation; it is found in all the ranks.

Tribal Religion in the American West

In the late 1880s, James Mooney (1860-1921), an ethnologist working for the Smithsonian Institute in Washington, traveled among the Native American tribes of the Plains seeking to do research on the Ghost Dance Religion. Mooney was sympathetic to the plight of the tribes at a time when few whites were so moved. In his study published by the Smithsonian in 1896, Mooney observed and even participated in some of the ritual dances, attempting to experience the moment from an insider's vantage point. In the selection below, the author records the hypnotic state that some participants experienced. Regarded as bizarre and threatening to many whites, the dance and the religion were suppressed by the U.S. government by 1890.

Source: James Mooney, *The Ghost-Dance Religion and the Sioux Outbreak of 1890*. Lincoln, Nebraska: University of Nebraska Press, 1991, pp. 925-926, originally published by the Government Printing Office, Washington, D.C., 1896.

We shall now describe the hypnotic process as used by the operators, with the various stages of the trance. The hypnotist, usually a man, stands within the ring, holding in his hand an eagle feather or a scarf or handkerchief, white, black, or of any other color. Sometimes he holds the feather in one hand and the scarf in the other. As the dancers circle around singing the songs in time with the dance step the excitement increases until the more sensitive ones are visibly affected. In order to hasten the result certain songs are sung to quicker time....We shall assume the subject is a woman. The first indication that she is being affected is a slight muscular tremor, distinctly felt by her two partners who hold her hands on either side. The medicine-man is on the watch, and as soon as he notices the woman's condition he comes over and stands immediately in front of her, looking intently into her face and whirling the feather or the handkerchief, or both, rapidly in front of her eyes, moving slowly around with the dancers at the same time, but constantly facing the woman. All this time he keeps up a series of sharp exclamations...like the rapid breathing of an exhausted runner. From time to time he changes the motion of the feather or handkerchief from a whirling to a rapid up-and-down movement in from [front] of her eyes. For a while the woman continues to move around with the circle of dancers, singing the song with others, but usually before the circuit is completed she loses control of herself entirely, and, breaking away from the partners who have hold of her hands on either side, she staggers into the ring, while the circle at once closes up again behind her. She is now standing before the medicine-man, who gives his whole attention to her, whirling the feather swiftly in from [front] of her eyes, waving his hands before her face as though fanning her, and drawing his hand slowly from the level of her eyes away to one side or upward into the air, while her gaze follows it with a fixed stare. All the time he keeps up the Hu! Hu! Hu! while the song and the dance go on around them without a pause. For a few minutes she continues to repeat the words of the song and keep time with the step, but in a staggering, drunken fashion. Then the words become unintelligible sounds, and her movements violently spasmodic, until at last she becomes rigid, with her eyes shut or fixed and staring, and stands thus uttering low pitiful moans. If this is in the daytime, the operator tries to stand with his back to the sun, so that the full sunlight shines in the woman's face. The subject may retain this, immovable posture for an indefinite time, but at last falls heavily to the ground, unconscious and motionless. The dance and the song never stop, but as soon as the woman falls the medicine-man gives his attention to another subject among the dancers. The first one may lie unconscious for ten or twenty minutes or sometimes for hours, but no one goes near her, as her soul is now communing with the spirit world. At last consciousness gradually returns. A violent tremor seizes her body as in the beginning of the fit. A low moan comes from her lips, and while she sits up and looks about her like one awaking from sleep. Her whole form trembles violently, but at last she arises to her feet and staggers away from the dancers, who open the circle to let her pass. All the phenomena of recovery, except rigidity, occur in direct reverse of those which precede unconsciousness.

A detail from the only known photo of the Lakota ghost dancers at Pine Ridge, 1890, three months prior to the killing of Sitting Bull. Photo by J. E. Meddaugh. (Courtesy of the Nebraska State Historical Society)

Sometimes before falling the hypnotized subject runs wildly about the circle or out over the prairie, or goes through various crazy evolutions like those of a lunatic. On one occasion—but only once—I have seen the medicine-man point his finger almost in the face of the hypnotized subject, and then withdrawing his finger describe with it a large circle about the tipis. The subject followed the direction indicated, sometimes being hidden from view by the crowd, and finally returned, with his eyes still fixed and staring, to the place where the medicine-man was standing. There is frequently a good deal of humbug mixed with these performances...but the greater portion is unquestionably genuine and beyond the control of the subjects. In many instances the hypnotized person spins around for minutes at a time like a dervish, or whirls the arms with apparently impossible speed, or assumes and retains until the final fall most uncomfortable positions which would be impossible to keep for any length of time under normal conditions. Frequently a number of persons are within the ring at once, in all the various stages of hypnotism.

Anti-Catholicism in America

Throughout much of the nineteenth century, American Catholics were plagued with written attacks from the Protestant majority. Oftentimes these attacks centered on what many Protestants saw as the seemingly irreconcilable differences between authoritarian Rome and American democracy. In most cases these works were not informed studies but were, instead, emotional diatribes against the Catholic Church. In the following account, the Rev. Isaac J. Lansing, a Protestant minister, delineates the dangers presented to American democratic institutions by the grasping Roman hierarchy, little of which is supported by empirical evidence.

Source: Isaac J. Lansing, *Romanism and the Republic: A Discussion of the Purposes, Assumptions, Principles and Methods of the Roman Catholic Hierarchy.* Boston: Arnold Publishing Association, 1896, pp. 25-37.

1. Why do I not take up and consider the relation of other churches to the Republic? That would be appropriate, if there were anything in their relation startling, threatening, or especially suggestive; but no such fact in their history exists.

   ....

2. It acknowledges as its head a ruler who claims the right to dictate to all rulers; who insists on his supremacy over and above all civil powers, executive and legislative....

   ....

3. The third reason why I consider the relations of Romanism and the Republic is, that Romanism hates and fiercely attacks institutions especially dear to us in this country, and which have been associated with all its prosperity from the beginning of our history....The system of public education has made, of those who

come under its benign influence, the most enlightened citizens of the most enlightened state in the world....But Rome is the sworn foe of our public schools. The most violent language in opposition to them is used, under the sanction of her prelates, by her writers, secular and clerical.

....

4. My fourth reason for considering Romanism in its relation to the Republic is, that in the Romish Church is so large a portion of the criminal and dangerous classes.

....

5. ...I beg you to remember, that already Rome acts in this country as a political unit. These dangerous elements, with all other elements of the Papal power, in their civil capacity, are wielded by the church as an adjunct of a single political party.

....

6. ...The power of the Papacy as a political force is already seen in our cities, not merely in the government of the municipality, nor in the blows which they are dealing at the public schools; but in those open violations of the constitution of the several states and of the United States, which they have extorted from time-serving legislators, and from trembling and subservient politicians.

....

7. My seventh reason is, that the leaders of the church, a celibate priesthood and without family ties, acknowledge an allegiance to a foreign ruler superior to the United States; and are already at his command....We cannot overlook the peculiarity of the Roman Catholic priesthood. It tends, contrary to nature and the law of God, to debase social morality. When the iron hand of the Papacy struck down the home of the priest by forbidding the priests to marry, it was that she might secure their more absolute allegiance to the church.

Toleration and Brotherhood: The World's Parliament of Religions

In 1893, as part of the Columbian Exposition in Chicago, many of the world's religious leaders gathered in a rare moment of brotherhood. The participants exchanged information, delivered papers on religious topics, and celebrated the universal attributes of the spiritual life that bound them. The gathering was unprecedented in world history and was a first step toward the ecumenism that would gain momentum in the twentieth century. In the reading below, Presbyterian John Henry Barrows, one of the major organizers of the World's Parliament of Religions, as it was called, reflects on the spirit of fraternity that marked the event.

Source: John Henry Barrows ed., *The World's Parliament of Religions*, vol. II. Chicago: The Parliament Publishing Company, 1893, pp. 1569-1570.

It is unwise to pronounce the Parliament, as some have done, a vindication or an illustration preeminently of one idea, either the Liberal, the Catholic, or the Evangelical. The Parliament was too large to be estimated and judged in this way. It did emphasize, as the Liberals have so emphatically done, liberty, fellowship, and character in religion; it did emphasize the Catholic idea of a universal church and the desirableness of greater unity in religious organization; it did emphasize and illustrate the great Evangelical claim that the historic Christ is divine, the sufficient and only Saviour of mankind; but from the fact that it made conspicuous so many truths and phases of religion, the glory of it cannot be monopolized by any one division of the religious world.

The echoes of the Parliament, reduplicated now in so many lands, show that it is destined to make a profound and ever-deepening impression on religious thought. It has shown that mankind is drifting toward religion and not away from it; it has widened the bounds of human fraternity; it is giving a strong impetus to the study of comparative religion; it is fortifying timid souls in regard to the right and wisdom of liberty in thought and expression; it is clarifying many minds in regard to the nature of non-Christian faiths; it is deepening the general Christian interest in non-Christian nations; and it will bring before millions in Oriental lands the more truthful and beautiful aspects of Christianity. The impression that is making on the unbelieving and secular world is salutary, for it gives the first opportunity for men to see religion in its entirety and to apprehend its greatness. The Columbia Exposition which accentuated the material glories of modern civilization needed the Parliament of Religions to bring back to the human mind the greater world of the Spirit.

The Congress was a notable event for the African, whose manhood was fully recognized; for the Jew, who has suffered various forms of persecution; for the Liberal, who saw the truths for which he has specifically contended grandly recognized; for the Catholic, who came out into a new atmosphere and gained from theological opponents new admiration and respect; for woman, for then she secured the largest recognition of her intellectual rights ever granted. It was a great event for the social reformer and advocate of international justice, for the Parliament was unanimous in denouncing the selfishness of modern society and the iniquity of the opium trade and the rum traffic; for the Buddhist, the Brahman and the Confucian, who were permitted to interpret their own faiths in the Parliament of Man; for the orthodox Protestant, whose heart and intellect were expanded and whose faith in the Gospels of God's grace was strengthened by the words and scenes of that assembly; and it was especially a great event for the earnest and broad-minded Christian missionary, who rejoiced that all Christendom was at last forced to confront the problem of bringing Christ, the universal Saviour, to all mankind.

Twentieth Century Struggles

Jehovah's Witnesses in Court - 1938

Can religious groups dispatch missionaries into neighborhoods and distribute literature and use recordings to promote their faith, even if these materials are offensive to members of other religious bodies? In Cantwell v. Connecticut *(1938), the U.S. Supreme Court answered in the affirmative. In the account that follows, readers will note the broad latitude the court grants in protecting the free exercise of religion, even to the point of protecting controversial groups and their teachings.*

Source: David Bollier, *Crusaders & Criminals, Victims & Visionaries: Historic Encounters Between Connecticut Citizens and the United States Supreme Court.* Hartford: Office of the Attorney General, 1986, pp. 44-46.

How far can the government go in telling someone how they can practice their religion? Newton Cantwell, devout member of the Jehovah's Witnesses group found out the hard way by getting arrested on the streets on New Haven in 1938 for practicing his religion. Ultimately, his case, *Cantwell v. Connecticut*, went on to become a landmark in our constitutional history—a case studied by every law student to illustrate how much religious freedom this nation enjoys under the First Amendment.

On April 26, 1938, Newton Cantwell and his wife, Esther, were practicing their ministry on Cassius Street in New Haven with two of their sons, Jesse and Russell, who were then 16 and 18 years old. As court records told the story, "Each was equipped with a bag containing books and pamphlets in several different languages, a portable phonograph, and a set of records each of which when played introduced and was a sales talk for one of the books. Their mode of operation was to go singly from house to house and ask permission to play one of the records."

One of the records was entitled "Enemies," and was an attack on the Catholic religion. What made this especially provocative was that 90 percent of the residents along Cassius Street were Roman Catholics. On Tuesday, April 28, 1938, as the Cantwells were going door-to-door, Jesse Cantwell played the record "Enemies" for two men he had stopped in the street. They told him to take his bag and victrola and leave, warning that they might beat him up if he didn't.

Russell Cantwell stopped at the home of Anna Rigby, a Catholic, and offered to sell her the book, "Riches." But she was already familiar with the book, which she considered an attack on her religion, and she got "mad enough to hit him if he did not go away." Even though Russell quietly left her house without an argument, Mrs. Rigby called the police.

....

The arrest was not entirely surprising. While Jehovah's Witnesses at the time had not encountered any trouble in their ministry in New Haven, police in New Britain, Bristol, Meriden, and other Connecticut communities had arrested about 300 Witnesses statewide. (Indeed both Newton and Jesse Cantwell had previously been arrested in either Bristol or New Britain, according to Russell Cantwell.)

Newton Cantwell and his sons were charged by New Haven police with breach of the peace. But they were also charged with violating a state law that prohibited citizens from soliciting money without a license—a charge that would later make the Cantwells' case a major constitutional issue. Under this law, it was illegal to solicit contributions for a religious cause or charity if one did not first obtain approval from the state. The law authorized the secretary of the public welfare council to decide whether a cause "is a religious one...."

The Jehovah's Witnesses refuse to let state authorities "approve" their religion, and so many police departments across the state arrested them for violating the solicitations law. According to Russell Cantwell, state prosecutors agreed to delay prosecuting the many cases until the status of the state law could be resolved by the courts. "Our case was selected to be a test case," said Russell Cantwell.

....

On May 20, 1940, the U.S. Supreme Court struck down the Connecticut solicitations law as a violation of the Cantwells "freedom of conscience" because the state was preventing them from practicing their religion. "Such a censorship of religion as the means of determining its right to survive is a denial of liberty protected by the First Amendment," the Court wrote. (It was the first time that the religious liberty clause of the First Amendment—which then only applied to the federal government—was applied to states and localities.)

The Court pointed out the difference between religious *belief* and religious *action*.

"The First Amendment embraces two concepts—freedom to believe and freedom to act. The first is absolute but, in the nature of things, the second cannot be. Conduct remains subject to regulation for the protection of society."

Thus, the state can regulate "the time, place and manner" of soliciting. And the state can "safeguard the peace, good order and comfort of the community." But the state cannot use its power to prevent someone from soliciting money simply because the state disapproves of that person's religion.

As for the breach of the peace charge, the Supreme Court overturned that as well. "We find...no assault or threatening of bodily harm, no truculent bearing, no intentional discourtesy, no personal abuse." The Court noted that the Cantwells' phonograph did not disturb the neighborhood, draw a crowd, or stop traffic. There was no "clear and present danger" of a riot or other violence.

Religious Toleration and the Presidency - 1960

While running for the presidency in 1960, John F. Kennedy encountered many questions regarding his ability to lead the nation while at the same time remain a faithful member of the Roman Catholic Church. Seeking to avoid the situation that plagued Democrat Al Smith in 1928, Kennedy agreed to address the Protestant Houston Ministerial Association in September of 1960, in an attempt to allay fears and correct misconceptions. The meeting proved to be a master stroke, as Kennedy skillfully satisfied the Association's queries. Below is an account of his address to Houston's Protestant clergy.

Source: *New York Times*, September 13, 1960, pp. 1, 22.

...because I am a Catholic, and no Catholic has ever been elected President, the real issues in this campaign have been obscured—perhaps deliberately, in some quarters less responsible than this. So it is apparently necessary for me to state once again—not what kind of church I believe in, for that should be important only to me, but what kind of America I believe in.

I believe in an America where the separation of church and state is absolute—where no Catholic prelate would tell the President (should he be a Catholic) how to act and no Protestant minister would tell his parishioners for whom to vote—where no church or church school is granted any public funds or political preference—and where no man is denied public office merely because his religion differs from the President who might appoint him or the people who might elect him.

I believe in an America that is officially neither Catholic, Protestant nor Jewish—where no public official either requests or accepts instructions on public policy from the Pope, the National Council of Churches or any other ecclesiastical source—where no religious body seeks to impose its will directly or indirectly upon the general populace or the public acts of its officials—and where religious liberty is so indivisible that an act against one church is treated as an act against all.

For, while this year it may be a Catholic against whom the finger of suspicion is pointed, in other years it has been, and someday may be again, a Jew—or a Quaker—or a Unitarian—or a Baptist. It was Virginia's harassment of Baptist preachers, for example, that led to Jefferson's statute of religious freedom. Today, I may be the victim—but tomorrow it may be you—until the whole fabric of our harmonious society is ripped apart at a time of great national peril.

Finally, I believe in an America where religious intolerance will someday end—where all men and all churches are treated as equal—where every man has the same right to attend or not to attend the church of his choice—where there is no Catholic vote, no anti-Catholic vote, no bloc voting of any kind—and where Catholics, Protestants and Jews, both the lay and the pastoral level, will refrain from those attitudes of disdain and division which have so often marred their works in the past and promote instead the American ideal of brotherhood.

That is the kind of America in which I believe. And it represents the kind of Presidency in which I believe—a great office that must be neither humbled by making it the instrument of any religious group, nor tarnished by arbitrarily withholding it, its occupancy from the members of any religious group. I believe in a President whose views on religion are his own private affair, neither imposed upon him by the nation or imposed upon him by the nation as a condition to holding that office.

Religion and the Public Schools - 1963

On June 17, 1963, Bible reading in public schools was declared unconstitutional. The U.S. Supreme Court ruling in Abington School District v. Schempp *argued that the opening of the school day in Abington, Pennsylvania—with a Bible reading—violated the Fourteenth Amendment. The Schempp family, which challenged the daily readings, had two children enrolled in school at the time. Below, Justice Tom Clark offers his reasons for striking down the Pennsylvania law.*

Source: Peter Irons and Stephanie Guitton eds., *May It Please the Court: Transcripts of 23 Live Recordings of Landmark Cases as Argued Before the Supreme Court.* New York: The New Press, 1993, pp. 70-71.

It is true that religion has been closely identified with our history and government....The fact that the Founding Fathers believed devotedly that there was a God and that the unalienable rights of man were rooted in Him is clearly evidenced in their writings, from the Mayflower Compact to the Constitution itself. This background is evidenced today in our public life through the continuance in our oaths of office from the Presidency to the Alderman of the final supplication, "So help me God." Likewise each House of the Congress provides through its Chaplain an opening prayer, and the sessions of this Court are declared open by the crier in a short ceremony, the final phrase of which invokes the grace of God....It can truly be said, therefore, that today, as in the beginning, our national life reflects a religious people who, in the words of Madison, are "earnestly praying, as...in duty bound, that the Supreme Lawgiver of the Universe...guide them into every measure which may be worthy of his blessing...."

This is not to say, however, that religion has been so identified with our history and government that religious freedom is not likewise as strongly embedded in our public and private life. Nothing but the most telling of personal experiences in religious prosecution suffered by our forebears,...could have planned our belief in liberty of religious opinion any more deeply in our heritage....The views of Madison and Jefferson, preceded by Roger Williams, came to be incorporated not only in the Federal Constitution but likewise in those of most of our States. This freedom to worship was indispensable in a country whose people came from the four quarters of the earth and brought with them a diversity of religious opinion. Today authorities list eighty-three separate bodies each with membership exceeding fifty thousand, existing among our people, as well as innumerable smaller groups....

First, this Court has decisively settled that the First Amendment's mandate that "Congress shall make no law respecting an establishment of religion, or prohibiting the free exercise thereof" has been wholly applicable to the States by the Fourteenth Amendment....

Second, this Court has rejected unequivocally the contention that the Establishment Clause forbids only governmental preference of one religion over another....

....

And in further elaboration the Court found that..."a union of government and religion tends to destroy government and to degrade religion."

The place of religion in our society is an exalted one, achieved through a long tradition of reliance on the home, the church and the inviolable citadel of the individual heart and mind. We have come to recognize through bitter experience that it is not within the power of government to invade that citadel, whether its purpose or effect be to aid or oppose, to advance or retard. In the relationship between man and religion, the State is firmly committed to a position of neutrality.

Black Muslims - 1965

Under the protection of religious freedom, there invariably emerge groups which have become controversial. The Nation of Islam, or Black Muslims, are one such body. Founded by W. D. Fard, a mysterious, itinerant peddler in Chicago in the 1930s, the Muslims have attracted attention by their advocacy of separatism, the occasional condemnation of other religious groups, their defiance of white culture, and their aloofness from American political life. The Nation's popularity peaked during the 1960s under the leadership of Elijah Muhammad (1896-1975). Below, Muhammad recalls his treatment in jail while serving a sentence for refusing to serve in World War II, a refusal he contends was based upon religious grounds.

Source: Elijah Muhammad, *Message to the Blackman in America.* Chicago: Muhammad's Temple No. 2, 1965, pp. 321-322.

On November 8, 1963, according to the *Chicago Tribune* newspaper, Federal Judge F. Ryan Duffy ruled that the Black Muslim "sect" is not a religion but is rather racist and has for its objective the overthrow of the white race. He further charged the believers of Islam inside prison walls as having a impressive history of inciting riots and violence.

I asked Judge Duffy to prove his charges. This is not true. In 1943, I was sent to the Federal Penitentiary in Milan, Michigan for nothing other than to be kept out of the public and from teaching my people the truth during the war between America, Germany, and Japan. This war came to a halt in 1945 when America dropped an atomic bomb on Japan. And the following year, in August, 1946, I was released on what the institution called "good time" for being a model prisoner who was obedient to the prison rules and laws.

In the year 1942-43, according to reports, there were nearly a hundred of my followers sentenced to prison terms of from 1 to 5 years for refusing to take part in the war between America, Japan, and Germany because of our peaceful stand and the principle belief and practice in Islam, which is peace.

The very dominant idea in Islam is the making of peace and not war; our refusing to go armed is our proof that we want peace. We felt that we had no right to take part in a war with nonbelievers of Islam who have always denied us justice and equal rights; and if we were going to be examples of peace and righteousness (as Allah has chosen us to be), we felt we had no right to join hands with the murderers of people or to help murder those who have done us no wrong. What would justify such actions? Let the truth answer.

Judge Duffy listened to an appeal made by a new convert to Islam who is serving a 200-year sentence, charged with slaying two Chicago men in 1951. (He should be given credit for his desire to be a Muslim). The appeal was asking for the freedom of obtaining publications and reading material distributed by the Black Muslims, including the Holy Quran [or Koran].

According to the rules and laws of the prison—before we Muslims began to be imprisoned—all religious believers, regardless to their religion and God, were permitted access to their books and visits by

Elijah Muhammad, the leader of the Black Muslims, had deep faith in Allah, the supreme being of Islam. (Courtesy of the National Archives)

their religious teachers. This freedom is written in the Constitution for everyone, but when we were imprisoned that freedom was denied us and us alone. And this is the freedom that is guaranteed in the American Constitution. A person is free to criticize anyone he wants, even if it is the Congress or President of the United States of America.

But while the Constitution of America was being written, our fathers were slaves, and we, today, are merely free slaves who do not have the knowledge of self and have not registered with Allah and His religion, the Nation of Islam.

When I was admitted into Cook County jail in Chicago, I wanted the Holy Qur-an, too, but I was denied having it, though it is not a "sect's Bible." It is the religious scriptures and guide for the Muslim world, recognized universally as the last revelation given to the world. And the Holy Qur-an has been the Holy Book and scripture for all Muslims for the past 1,381 years.

We are not an organization; we are a world. I use the same Holy Qur-an that all Muslims use; the book that is universally recognized as being 100 per cent true. And such scholar and U.S. Judge as F. Ryan Duffy calls it a "sect's book."

One of the officers, who was a very fine man, tried in vain to persuade the warden in the Cook County jail to allow me to have my Holy Qur-an as other religious believers were receiving theirs in prison. But this same officer came back and told me that the warden said "That is what we put them in prison for, and to let us read the Bible, ha, ha, ha."

Peyote and Native American Freedom of Religion - 1992

One of the most sensitive issues facing the courts in recent times is determining the legality in the use of peyote, a cactus grown in a small area of eastern Mexico and western Texas. Peyote bears a fruit that, when eaten, produces an hallucinogenic effect. Native Americans in the West have argued that their use of the plant in religious ceremonies predates the coming of Columbus and is prized only for its sacramental use. Conversely, government officials have called attention to its potentially mind-altering properties and have argued for control over its cultivation, distribution, and usage. In the account below, testimony as to the plant's origins is given at a Senate Hearing in 1992. The mythic aspect of the testimony, while considered sacred to Native Americans, might appear wholly-unfounded to government officials, only adding further complexity to the issue of religious freedom.

The use of peyote is permitted today in the worship services of the Native American Church of North America, but is closely scrutinized by government authorities.

Source: "Testimony of Truman Dailey, Native American Church of Oklahoma," Religious Freedom Act: *Hearing; Select Committee on Indian Affairs, United States Senate, One Hundred and Second Congress, Second Session*, March 7, 1992. Portland Oregon, pp. 257-259.

From the beginning of time a woman found this medicine commonly known as peyote. Naturally we do not know how long ago this took place. There is always a beginning of everything. Christianity had its start when Jesus Christ was born. Today there are many religious denominations and each one believes in the teaching of Jesus Christ. Likewise, this Native American Church had its beginning.

The woman that discovered the peyote went alone with the warriors of her tribe. They went out to scout the area to see if there were any danger or enemies. In doing so they encountered an enemy tribe. The results of this warfare the enemy killed all the warriors she was with. Before the battle took place the warriors hid her so the enemy would not capture her. After the enemy left this woman found herself all alone. She did not know what direction they came from. She began to wonder around. She did not have any food or water to drink. Finally she fell to the ground through exhaustion. Naturally being weak she went to sleep. I may add here that Indians believe in visions or dreams of a certain nature. In her weakness she was trying to grab something to eat. She grabbed things and brought them to her mouth to eat. Finally she grabbed something that was soft and pulpy. She put it to her mouth and it was edible. It had lots of juice and it quenched her thirst and hunger. The peyote had strange and mysterious effects. She began her dream or vision. There was a bird came and flew and stayed right above her. According to the story the bird told her to get up and go a certain direction and those people would help her. She arose and went in that direction. She found a type of dwelling, and there were people inside. One man came out and told her that they were expecting her. So they invited her inside this dwelling. When she got seated seven men dressed in their ceremonial clothes. They asked her to express herself if she had any problems. After telling all she went through they told her to look at the fire where the fireplace is and have her mind and thoughts focused toward the fireplace. Whatever is on your mind you may be blessed to see. Through the brilliant blaze of the fire there appeared the faces one at a time of the warriors she was with. Each one showed no expression of pain or sadness. Their expression on their face was happiness. The ceremony she was in they followed their regular routine. Each man sang four songs. They had a drum to create the rhythm and they invited her to help them as they sang their songs. She was in this spiritual ceremony until it was all over. The leader gave her instructions and told her when you step outside you go in that direction and don't leave it until you find your people. When she stepped outside she woke up. She was still lying where she fell. This is what she went through. This was caused by the strange effects of the peyote.

The peyote helps us in whatever is on our mind. We receive comfort, knowledge and wisdom and many other good things that we want to accomplish. When this woman arose, she gathered as much peyote as she could carry.

She started her journey to find her people....she told the experience she went through when she ate the peyote. The tribe...did not pay much attention to her story. Several years went by and a terrible epidemic invaded the tribe. People were dying. The leaders of the tribe were at a loss....Someone thought of this woman....They backtracked until they found the fields of peyote. They gathered much of it and took it back to the village. Before eating the peyote the people prayed and several days time they began to get well....In the passing of time the people developed a ceremony, they found that the best time to have this ceremony was during the night....From that time until now it has been developed into a beautiful religious ceremony.

Religious Dissent:
A Commentary

Dissent has played an important role in American religious history. In the following excerpt, historian Edwin Scott Gaustad discusses this role. Of critical importance is the contribution dissent has made to the nation's religious pluralism.

Source: Edwin Scott Gaustad, *Dissent in American Religion.* Chicago: University of Chicago Press, 1973, pp. 3-4.

The American experiment,...was to place both orthodoxy and dissent upon the same shifting platforms of public favor and public support. Throughout so much of American history, it has been distressingly difficult to separate the "ins" from the "outs": What was stubborn schism in Massachusetts was quiet conformity in Virginia; what was doctrinal sobriety in Pennsylvania was intolerable in Connecticut; what was proper churchmanship in Rhode Island was arrogant pretension almost everywhere else. E pluribus unum in American history? Hardly. Not only was there wild diversity in space, there was unsettling instability in time. The conformity so rigidly demanded in the seventeenth century was largely forgotten in the eighteenth. What was theological error for one generation was for the next a vaguely disquieting dream. That which one age was willing to die for another age was not prepared to live for. And then deliberate disestablishment with the adoption of the First Amendment in 1791, further confounding the contrary categories of orthodoxy and dissent, of respectability and heresy, of decency and order against impropriety and sectarian novelty. The lions might be thirsty for blood, but where should they turn. So the confusions concerning good order, right opinion, and agreeable behavior continued until the vices of dissent were seen as virtues and the glories of pluralism were heralded as the American Way of Life. Up to a point.

For if society is diverse, flexible, adaptive, and pragmatic, why do we still hear quarrelsome cries of dissent? Why cannot everybody cooperate, get along, play the game, work within the system? Why multitudes still so unmelted, still so unwashed? Why the long lines of detractors and despisers, the sweaty crowds of nay-sayers and protesters? Is it possible that dissent is something more than flexible adaptability, that the abandonment of "creeds outworn" is not its full message? It is possible to gain the "free world" and nonetheless lose one's soul? Dissent cannot be understood simply in terms of whines against oppression, resistance to organizational corruption, demurrers against the affirmations of others. To view dissent in these terms is to suppose that when all external restraints are removed and all ecclesiastical authority stilled, then dissent falls flat on its face never to rise again. This could be the case only if dissenters were merely noisy nay-sayers.

But history hones dissent to a fine edge; sharp, severe, unyielding. While it is true that restraint and oppression frequently give dissent its cohesion and therefore its strength as a mass movement, it is not true that, apart from these external forces, the dissenter is without aim or energy or nerve. Rather, the dissenter is a powerful if unpredictable engine in the service of a cause. Though he is prone to many sins, sloth is not his crime. The path of greatest resistance is frequently the very one that the dissenter sets himself upon. He may cast out demons dwelling in others; himself he cannot save.

One might argue that the above describes not the dissenting man but the religious man, *homo religiosus*. This observation has some validity. Religion in its essence is already offbeat, irregular, asymmetric. It confronts and attempts to cope with the unexpected and the unexplained. That which conforms, that which is balanced, that which is orderly and precise does not require the ministrations of cult or clergy, of ritual or myth. The profoundly religious man resists the routine, defies the machine, confounds the computer....he is concerned not with process but with event. Yet, as everyone knows, religious institutions do make their peace with the world, they do themselves become part of the regular order. So the prophet contends with the priest, protests the accommodations, calls forth fresh energies, and challenges the unfeeling stones within existing structures. This reform of religion in the name of religion, this growing edge, this refusal to let well-enough alone, is the role of dissent.

Suggested Further Reading

In addition to the works cited in the text, the following books are also recommended.

Austin, Allan D. *African Muslims in Antebellum America.* New York: Routledge, 1997.

Brant, Irving. *The Bill of Rights: Its Origin and Meaning.* Indianapolis: Bobbs-Merrill, 1965.

Connors, Eugene T. *Religion and the Schools: Significant Court Decisions in the 1980s.* Bloomington, Indiana: Phi Delta Kappa Educational Foundation, 1988.

Greene, Evarts B. *Religion and the State: The Making and Testing of an American Tradition.* Ithaca: Cornell University Press, 1941.

Lanternari, Vittorio. *The Religions of the Oppressed: A Study of Modern Messianic Cults.* New York: The New American Library, 1963.

Levy, Leonard W. *The Establishment Clause: Religion and the First Amendment.* New York: Macmillan Publishing Company, 1986.

Kinzer, David L. *An Episode in Anti-Catholicism: The American Protective Association.* Seattle: University of Washington Press, 1964.

Morgan, Richard E. Morgan. *The Politics of Religious Conflict.* New York: Western Publishing Company, Inc., 1968.

Murray, John Courtney. *We Hold These Truths: Catholic Reflections on the American Proposition.* New York: Sheed and Ward, 1960.

Raab, Earl ed. *Religious Conflict in America: Studies in the Problem Beyond Bigotry.* New York: Doubleday & Company, 1964.

Stewart, Omer, C. *Peyote Religion: A History.* Norman: University of Oklahoma Press, 1987.

Tavel, David. *Church-State Issues in Education.* Bloomington, Indiana: Phi Delta Kappa Educational Foundation, 1979.

Wilson, John F, ed. *Church and State in America.* Englewood, New Jersey: D.C. Heath and Company, 1965.

Also of interest from the *Perspectives on History Series*, Discovery Enterprises, Ltd., Carlisle, MA:

Coleman, Wim. *The Quakers.* 1997.

— *The Shakers.* 1997.

Emert, Phyllis Raybin. *The Missions of California.* 1997

Foley, Shelia. *Faith Unfurled: The Pilgrims' Quest for Freedom.* 1993.

Knapp-Sawyer, Kem. *Pennsylvania Dutch: The Amish and the Mennonites.* 1997.

Find out about other topics in the *Perspectives on History Series* by calling for a free catalog at 1-800-729-1720 or write to: Discovery Enterprises, Ltd., 31 Laurelwood Drive, Carlisle, MA 01741.